SCHIRMER'S LIBRARY OF MUSICAL CLASSICS

WOLFGANG AMADEUS MOZART

Concertos

For the Piano

Critically Revised, Fingered, and
the Orchestral Accompaniments
Arranged for a Second Piano

G. SCHIRMER, Inc.

DISTRIBUTED BY

HAL•LEONARD®
CORPORATION

7777 W. BLUEMOUND RD. P.O. BOX 13819 MILWAUKEE, WI 53213

PREFACE

The principal source for this edition of the C-major Concerto was the autograph of the score, belonging to Conductor-in-Chief W. Taubert. Besides the above, I collated the old Breitkopf & Härtel edition of the parts, an early André engraved edition of the piano-part, Richault's score-edition, the score-edition published by André* in 1855, the new Breitkopf & Härtel edition of the score (Series XVI, 21), and other modern editions.

The autograph is dated "Febraio 1785." Although it contains many passages which are "written over," the text is, with few exceptions, nowhere doubtful. Some disputed points are discussed in the Notes. The following peculiarities in the autograph have not been adhered to in the present edition:

(1) As staccato-marks we find in part dashes, in part dots. But it does not appear to have been the composer's intention to indicate different degrees of abbreviation.

(2) The short appoggiaturas, counting among them those which, in the livelier movements, admit of an execution as sixteenth-notes, are written as small sixteenth-notes, or (more rarely) as thirty-second-notes. There is no apparent reason for making a distinction between the two. The relatively long appoggiaturas in the Andante are given in our text, in conformity with the autograph, as eighth-notes.

(3) In the Tutti the direction "col Basso" is almost invariably given in the cembalo-part. As this direction has become meaningless in our day, there had to be made, at the closes of some of the Soli, certain slight alterations, giving to both right hand and left a quarter-note for the last chord; whereas Mozart had written an eighth-note for the connection with the orchestral bass. It should be observed that early editions do not always notice the places where the direction "col Basso" is intentionally omitted.

Below are quoted a series of earlier readings, which later made way for the versions contained in our text:

Page 5, staff 14, measures 2–5, and p. 6, st. 2, meas. 1. Originally, the second half of each measure in the bass read like the first half, which gave rise to various bad leadings of the parts.

Page 6, st. 10, meas. 1. Figure in the bass:

* Wherever André is quoted, without special qualification, the score-edition is meant.

Page II, st. I, meas. I. Earlier form:

Page II, st. 6, meas. 2 and 3. Originally, both hands played in octaves, thus:

The accompaniment by the string-quartet, requiring a change in the passage, appears to have been added later.

Page 14, st. 5, meas. 4. The last beat read, originally:

that is, *g'* instead of *f'*. Corresponding deviations 2 and 4 measures further on. Correction finally indistinct.

Page 18, st. I and 2, meas. 2. At first written in both staves an octave higher.

Page 20, st. 2, meas. 6, and st. 6, meas. I. Originally, the left hand played *unisono* with the bassoon-parts.

Page 23 *et seq.* In the Andante the accompanying parts were frequently refined by later corrections. From the 12th measure onward the bass originally read:

Page 32, st. I, meas. 3 and 5. At first the viola-part read:

Later, in consideration of the *e'♭* in the piano-part, the half-note *g'* was substituted. Here the score-editions are at fault.

Page 37, st. 2, meas. 7 and 8. The bass figure was written at first an octave higher.

All *heavily* engraved slurs, dots and expression-marks are found in the autograph. The editor's additions are distinguishable by lighter (or smaller) engraving.

To Messrs. Conductor-in-Chief Taubert, Royal Librarian Dr. Kopfermann, and Dr. Erich Prieger, special thanks are due for so kindly furnishing material for the revision of the text.

DR. HANS BISCHOFF.

Berlin, 1886.

W. A. Mozart.
CONCERTO
in C major

W. A. Mozart.
CONCERTO
in C major
for the Pianoforte.

Played by the composer on March 12, 1785.

Pianoforte II.

(1) The tempo-mark is wanting in the autograph.

(2) The autograph gives *a* on the third beat; at the repetition by the Tutti in the further course of the movement, *g* is given. Either is possible. Published editions either follow the autograph exactly, or give in both places either *a* or *g*.

Printed in the U.S.A.

Cadenza by August Winding.

(3) In Richault, in the old Br. & H. edition, etc., etc., there is a turn-sign over *b*¹.

(4) Several editions (Richault, Peters, etc.) have an inverted mordent (Pralltriller) at *a*², and also at the corresponding note in the second measure but one following. The old Br. & H. edition gives a 𝄎 in that place.

(5) The tie at *d* is omitted in the autograph.

(6) In the new Br. & H. score, and other editions, the appoggiaturas are read as sixteenth-notes proportionally distributed in the measure; a mode of performance which, though permissible, is not unconditionally acceptable.

(7) d²♯ for d² in the old André edition.

(8) Compare the earlier form of this measure as quoted in the Preface. The alteration in the bass caused the composer to give up the dotted rhythm of the highest part; several editions (the old Br. & H., André, Richault, Peters) retain it.

(9) Here, and for the eighth sixteenth-note in the next measure, some recent editions wrongly read *c* for *c♯*.

(10) The new Br. & H. score gives wrongly c♯ for c.

(11) Here the staccatos are indicated in the autograph by dashes. As observed in the Preface, I do not, attempt to distinguish between dashes and dots, as the autograph exhibits no consistency in this point.

(14) The score-editions of Richault and André read incorrectly *g* instead of *b*. See the parallel passage in *G*. The autograph is not quite distinct.

(15) The direction "col Basso" is wanting here in the cembalo-part. Nevertheless, old editions carry on the bass.
(16) There is no ♮ in the autograph. But the parallel passage shows that the frequent reading ♭♭ instead of ♭ is wrong.

(17) The afterbeat was forgotten in autograph.

(18) The Lebert edition, which on the whole pursues lines other than those of pure and simple textual criticism, reads as follows in this passage:

Cadenza by A. Winding.

(1) The direction "pizzicato" is omitted in the Br. & H. score-edition.
(2) In Richault, and the old Br. & H. edition of the parts, we find *e g* instead of *g b♭*. See the remark, in the Preface, on the earlier reading of this passage.

(3) In consequence of a misinterpreted abbreviation in the autograph, several editions (*e.g.*, Richault, Peters, and the old Br. & H. issue) read, instead of the two half-notes, one whole note, *a*. Similar mistakes occur frequently in other places.
(4) Richault, André, and others, omit the afterbeat.

(5) In this figure, and others of like form, it is not plain whether the slur should extend over two or three eighth-notes
(6) The chromatic signs with which the turns are provided, were added by the editor.
(7) These small signs, and the small notes in parenthesis, are given in Richault and the old Br. & H. edition of the
parts. They are lacking in the autograph.

(8) The Br. & H. score does not sufficiently distinguish between long and short appoggiaturas. For the time-value
of this *e♯* the editor proposes that of a simple eighth-note.
(9) In this and all similar passages the autograph originally gave, not the Fourth, but the Third. See Preface.

(10) See Note 3.

(11) According to the old Br. & H. edition of the parts, and Richault, the chord also contains the note *d*. This reading is also found in recent issues. The autograph is indistinct.

(12) In the editions just mentioned, the note *B* is lacking.

(13) See Note 3.

Allegro vivace assai.

Cadenza by A. Winding.

(1) While the direction "col Basso" had been in force down to this point, the piano-part in the autograph continues thus:

(2) In Richault, and some modern editions, *a* instead of *g*.

(3) Engraver's error in the Br. & H. score; also in the Reinecke edition.

Cadenza by A. Winding.

(4) In the autograph, the connection with the orchestral bass reads: See Preface.

(5) The score-editions read e^1 instead of d^1 as the second eighth-note in the 2d violins.

(6) In the next 15 measures the autograph exhibits inaccuracies in the notation of the staccato. The Br. & H. score adds, in some places, unauthorized slurs.

(7) In the old Br. & H. edition the next four eighth-notes are omitted.

(8) Frequent Variant:

(9) The *c* in the bass is omitted in the new Br. & H. score.

(10) Richault, and the old Br. & H. edition of the piano-part, give both times b^2 instead of b^2b.

(11) In conformity with the autograph, many editions do not give the ♯ before f^2 until the third eighth-note. Probably a slip of the pen was made here.

Solo Cadenza by A. Winding.

(12) Several editions have filling chords in the **upper staff.**